COLOR
100
HAPPY
PASSAGES

To Daniel, Almerinda, and Coskun.

Thunder Bay Press
An imprint of Printers Row Publishing Group
10350 Barnes Canyon Road, Suite 100, San Diego, CA 92121
www.thunderbaybooks.com • mail@thunderbaybooks.com

Correspondence regarding the content of this book should be sent to Thunder Bay Press,
Editorial Department, at the above address. Author and illustration inquiries should be
addressed to Éditions First, an imprint of Édi8, 12 avenue d'Italie, 75013 Paris, France.

Publisher: Peter Norton
Publishing Team: Lori Asbury, Ana Parker, Laura Vignale, Stephanie Romero Gamboa
Editorial Team: JoAnn Padgett, Melinda Allman, Dan Mansfield
Production Team: Jonathan Lopes, Rusty von Dyl

ISBN: 978-1-64517-209-3

Printed in China

23 22 21 20 19   2 3 4 5 6

COLOR
100
HAPPY
PASSAGES

LISA MAGANO
CHARLOTTE LEGRIS

THUNDER BAY
P·R·E·S·S

San Diego, California

Lisa's tips

With colored pencils

Using colored pencils allows you to create fine gradations,
and to come up with your own shades by mixing colors.
Soft pencils are best. The rule for a smooth color: always color
in the same direction without going back and forth,
and apply several light layers.

With felt-tips

The point can be large, medium, or fine—have fun mixing and
matching! Just some advice: don't press the point too hard on
the page, and don't go over the same area several times.

And a warning: felt-tips containing alcohol,
whatever the brand, seep through the pages.

With watercolor pencils or marker

Simply color, then go over the area of your choice with
a moistened brush to turn it into a watercolor.
Be careful—if the brush is too wet the pages will warp.
Remember to rinse your brush before using it on another color.

Today's defeat is tomorrow's victory.

The path is the destination. Enjoy the journey.

When you share your happiness, it grows.

Rain is the promise of sun.

look at the sky to elevate your soul.

Listen to the silence.

Letting go means focusing on the essential.

LIVE EACH DAY LIKE AN ENTIRE LIFETIME.

DO WHAT you love TO love WHAT you DO.

Only dead leaves go with the wind.

TODAY
I WILL CHOOSE
JOY.

Every life
has a purpose.

live for today,
hope for tomorrow.

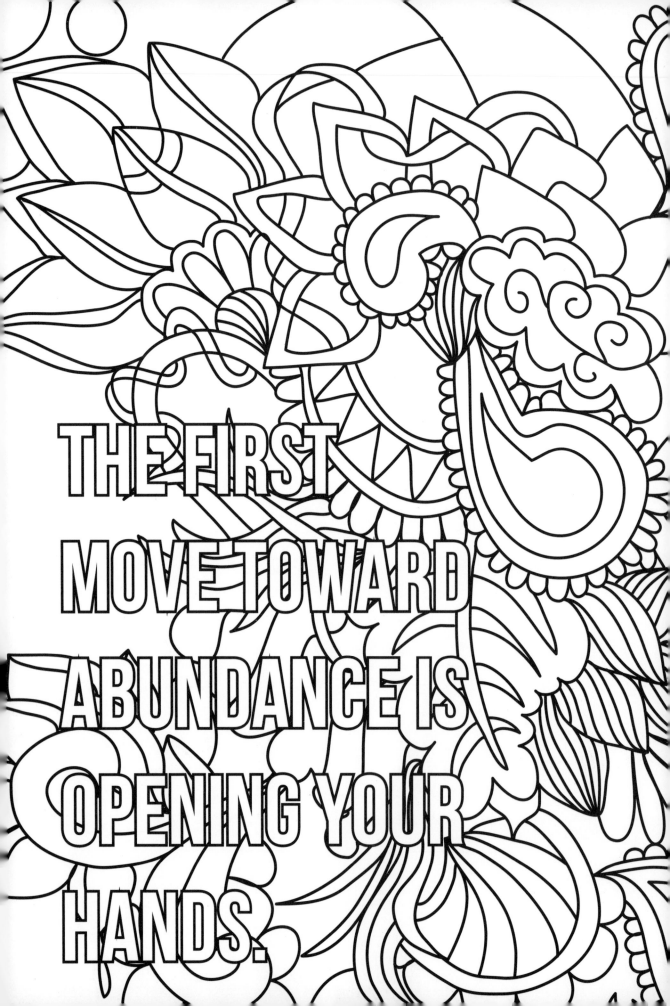

Decide to be happy.

Simplicity is the greatest wealth.

Look within for happiness—nowhere else.

My destiny is my life's work.

Your daily life is a treasure. Guard it carefully.

The power of amazement.

STOP WAITING FOR THE STORM TO END; ADMIRE THE LIGHTNING.

When you laugh every day, you're taking good care of yourself.

YOU NEED TALENT TO SUCCEED— BUT MOSTLY COURAGE.

Use your life to become yourself.

What can I do to make others happy?

life smiles on optimists.

I am present in the world.

I breathe, I am. I am.

I breathe, therefore I am.

therefore I breathe.

I breathe, therefore I am.

Dialogue can change everything.

You can never express too much gratitude.

Tear down the walls and open the doors of your mind.

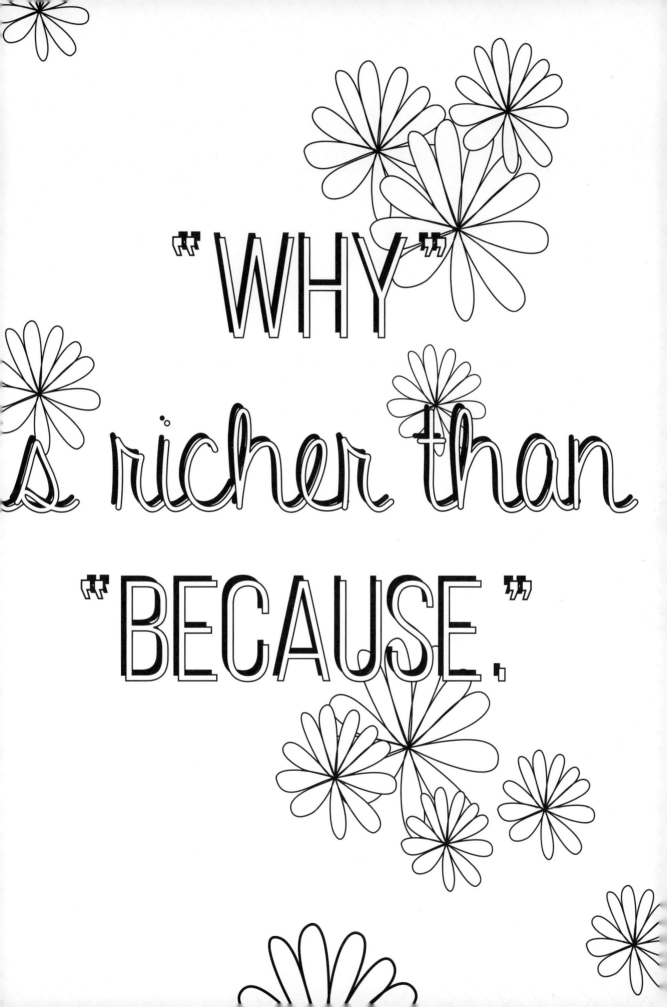

"WHY" is richer than "BECAUSE."

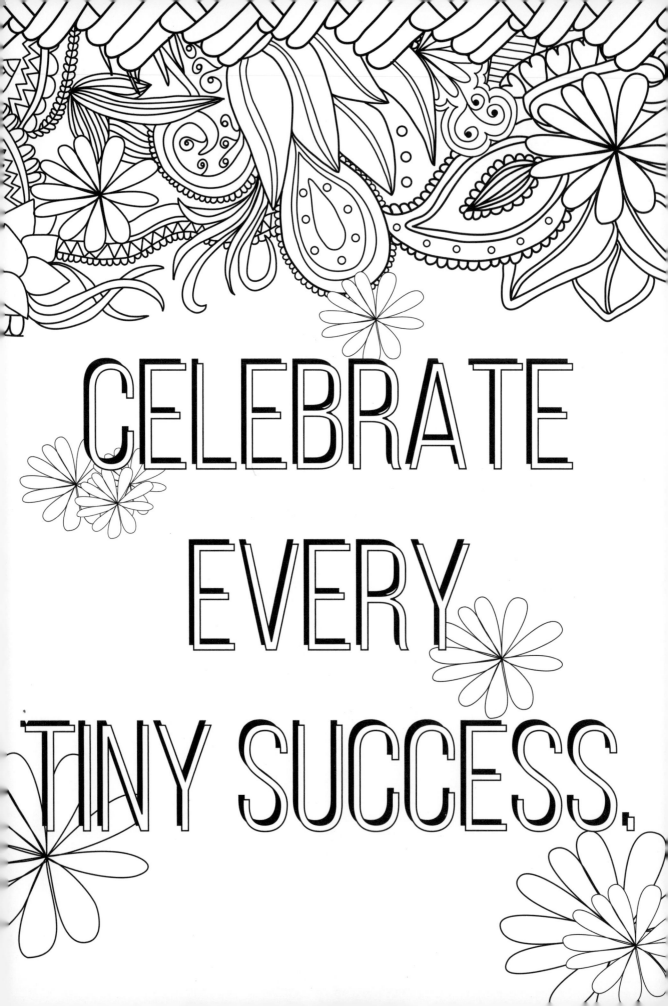

You travel farther without baggage.

Kindness forges the strongest bonds.

Imagination is an unalienable right.

Love can
do it all.

Courage can do it all.

Luck is the skill to spot opportunities.

Happiness is a state of mind.

Lie on the grass and look at the sky.

FOR A RADIANT FUTURE, TAKE GOOD CARE OF THE PRESENT.

Some things are not important. Move on.

IF
you want to
CHANGE
the world,
CHANGE
yourself.

Smiling is a universal language.

Turn anger into energy.

NOTHING is POSSIBLE without THOUGHT, and THOUGHT makes everything POSSIBLE.

It is sometimes useful to do useless things.

Not trying is more painful than regret.

Accepting our weaknesses
makes us stronger.

It is never too late for self-realization.

When you look out for others,
you look out for yourself.

TO CONQUER FEAR, ACT.

Live your life—it's unique.

Say "Why not?" instead of "Why?"

We are nourished by beauty.

Trust is calming.

THE FACE
ACLES
give up
REEDOM.

Turn anger into energy.

Don't predict the future,
invent it.

The truth will always prevail.

let go of regrets.

The heart speaks all languages.

We are all miracles.

Make peace with yourself.

TO FEEL IS TO BE ALIVE.

I nurture my inner light.

We always have a choice.

It is okay to ask for help.

You're the artist!